Confidence
Within

Authentic Confidence for Women

Anne McGhee
The *Can-Do* Coach for Women

Paperback ISBN 9781780922799
ePub ISBN 9781780922805
PDF ISBN 9781780922812

Published in the UK by MX Publishing
335 Princess Park Manor, Royal Drive,
London, N11 3GX
www.mxpublishing.com

Cover design by www.staunch.com

"I was always looking outside myself for strength and confidence, but it comes from within. It is there all the time." Anna Freud

Acknowledgements

With love and gratitude I acknowledge

My parents, Elizabeth and George McGhee whose belief in me has never wavered, if on a soul level we choose our parents, I chose well – thank you!

My siblings, Frances, Sandra and George for their encouragement and support through tough times.

My Mentor, Alexandra Watson for her support, guidance and motivation during the writing of this book.

Anne Marie McIntosh, Executive Coach and friend for her promptness in reading the first draft of this book, her encouraging and enthusiastic feedback.

My clients, for their courage to close the confidence competence gap, step up and into their personal and professional best. You inspire me! A special thanks to those who were willing and gave permission to share their experiences, insights and learning.

Content

Introduction   6

About the Author – A bit about me and my journey   8

Chapter 1 – Authentic Confidence   11

Chapter 2 – Unpacking the Baggage from the Past   30

Chapter 3 – You're not the girl you think you are   50

Chapter 4 - The Importance of Self-Honour   60

Chapter 5 – Self-Care   71

Chapter 6 – Developing Your Confidence
              Resource Kit   79

Chapter 7 – Your Word Is Your Wand or Is It?   92

Chapter 8 – Can you? - You CAN!   103

Introduction

Confidence is a bit like a pendulum swinging from one extreme to another. It's in a constant state of flux for everyone, believe me, I've coached enough people to know this, nobody and I mean nobody is confident all the time and in every situation.

But there can come a time at any point in one's life, no matter how outwardly successful you are or perceived to be, you just don't feel it on the inside. You feel like a fraud, an imposter and you fear that you're going to get found out. Your confidence lags behind your competence.

Been there, done that, and I know only too well how horribly debilitating that can be. I remember feeling completely disconnected to the female staring back at me in the mirror, she looked good, she walked and talked with confidence but inside I felt empty and fearful of being found out, because **I** didn't believe in **me** and doubted the words of others who did.

I am sure there will be people who know me, who will be surprised to get that insight because outwardly I appeared very together. Seeing others achieve in a way I desired but being frozen by fear I had to learn and develop confidence crisis strategies that worked when required, but authentic confidence only came when I learned to accept and value myself and connect with my inner wisdom.

The purpose of this book, whilst containing a fusion of confidence boosting tips and techniques, is to take you on a journey of self-re-discovery. We'll start by examining what confidence really is, how it affects our perceptions; of ourselves, our capabilities and others. How confidence can work for us and against us in situations and the attributes and attraction of natural confidence.

I'll provide you with a road map to get to that authentic place, where you accept and appreciate yourself, a place from which you can develop confidence within and learn to prosper. You will learn how to acknowledge and process your past so that you can leave the baggage and the limiting beliefs behind and use the insights and learning gained from it to inform, step up and into your desired future.

I aim to take you to that place where you learn to honour yourself, where you see the power of daring to dream and where you give yourself permission to believe; you can be who you want to be and get what you want out of life. You will learn to recognise your resilience and develop your personal resources for life lasting confidence and most importantly to trust your inner wisdom and that still, small voice within that whispers, "You CAN DO It."

A bit about me and my journey

My entire career has revolved around working with people, helping them to see and develop their own potential. Firstly, I worked as a secondary school guidance teacher with young people and then moved into the management and delivery of professional and personal development programmes for staff in the public and private sector.

Five years ago, I was made redundant from my post as contract manager with a training company. Whilst I was happy to move on from that position, I hadn't realised how much of my identity was tied up in it or how being unemployed, and the challenges it brought, would affect my confidence.

I had a good professional reputation, but I lacked direction. I felt lost and thought that I lacked options although that was not really true. I was getting interviews but I was sabotaging them, but not really understanding why. On reflection, I think deep down my desire to run my own business was probably stronger than even I was conscious of.

I trained as a professional coach and set up my coaching and consultancy business which brought with it a whole load of other challenges to my confidence; networking, pitching, tendering and negotiating fees. None of these skills were new to me but I lacked the confidence to make that connection and to transfer the skills I was competent in to my new business.

If I'm being honest, I took any form of rejection personally. I lacked self-belief and was often confused and even horrified by those who did believe in me. The gap between my confidence and my competence was so huge that I was always looking for a plan B just in case my business failed. With another business women I set up a business network, which I ran successfully for two years. I trained as a Pilates instructor – neither of which was easy, believe me!

Yet I still lacked self-esteem and belief in my ability to achieve my ambitions and see myself as a success. I was always seeking approval, permission and validation from others about my worth and capabilities. At the time I thought I was alone in feeling this way, what I've learned is that most women feel this way at some point.

I've read loads of books on personal, professional and spiritual development. I've employed coaches, attended hundreds of training courses, webinars as well as being a member of online forums and a mastermind group to help me in my quest to close the confidence-competence gap. But it was only when I did the inner work and reconnected to my feminine wisdom that I was led to a place of trust, peace, balance and wellbeing. Confident in who I am and what I have to offer is of value.

What I've learned is that being confident is about knowing;

- Who you are.
- What it is you stand for.
- What it is that's important for you to be, to do and to have in life.

It's about recognising and reclaiming your worth and wisdom. Authentic confidence is a 'felt sense' of trust in your innate self and the universal truth that all is well and whatever life throws at you - you can handle it and whatever you want to achieve 'You CAN DO It!'

Chapter 1 – Authentic Confidence

Confidence – *the quality of being certain of your abilities or of having trust in people, plans, or the future.*

The Cambridge Dictionary

Confidence is complex; a chameleon - it changes according to what's going on in our life, the situations in which we find ourselves and even who we are with. A sought after and desirable quality, yet according to its measure it can be a friend or foe and is often a master of disguise.

Desirable

Confidence is spellbinding, ageless, seductive and a certain kind of sexy. We can find ourselves attracted to the most unlikely folk, simply because they are comfortable in their own skin. I remember many years ago being amused and if I'm honest confused to hear a colleague of mine refer to the actor Jack Nicholson as being 'dead sexy'. Not your usual movie hunk but it was his self-assurance she found so alluring. I recall reading an article a while back about the actress Francesca Annis who at the age of 61 was being described as 'still sexy' not because of her looks although still a very attractive woman, but more because of her attitude and self-belief.

Friend

When we feel confident we tend to deal with a situation or the task in hand in a state of flow often barely conscious of what we are doing and perhaps even what we are achieving. The right amount of confidence allows us to answer the door to opportunity when it knock's and knock on doors when they are closed. Even if the doors are shut in our face confidence allows us to try another door or walk a completely different path.

Foe

There are times however, when we can be over confident in ourselves and in our abilities and this can lead to arrogance, complacency and even recklessness. Considering yourself more intelligent, more skilled or more competent than a fellow team member is arrogant. Not preparing sufficiently for an interview you think is in the bag is reckless. Speaking to or treating your partner inappropriately, because you think he'll never leave you, is complacent.

Master of disguise

A lack of confidence can also be acted out and interpreted as aloofness and even aggressiveness as we employ strategies to protect ourselves from showing our weaknesses and minimise our discomfort.

It's not uncommon for a shy person who runs an internal script of 'why would they want to talk to me' to be thought of as rude or anti-social. They come across as unapproachable. They avoid eye contact and are unable to engage in general chit chat. Yet, inside they are dying with discomfort and desperately wanting to be something different; a confident conversationalist.

Not everyone who lacks confidence is shy. Until recently I would have included myself in that group. I was able to stand in front of large audiences and give presentations, yet at the same time suffer from the Imposter Syndrome fearing I would get caught out because my confidence lagged behind my competence.

The Imposter Syndrome is a widespread phenomenon identified more than 30 years ago by clinical psychologists Pauline Clance and Suzanne Imes. It defines and describes feelings of being inauthentic in your role, feeling unworthy of the recognition or compensation you receive you feel like a fraud. The consequences of these feelings are many, not voicing your opinions or sharing your ideas, not asking for a raise or promoting yourself. These behaviours can fuel failure and frustration, emotionally strangling suffers and derailing their career because they won't give themselves the permission to discover and demonstrate the leader within.

On the other end of the spectrum, instead of acting passively some women adopt a more masculine approach and become overly aggressive. In the 2011 series of *The Apprentice* one of the contestants, Melody Hossaini, in an interview at the end of the series commented that a key learning for her from participating in the programme was that when she felt vulnerable she became very aggressive; a self-protection mechanism to hide her lack of confidence. She now realises that becoming comfortable with her vulnerability and being able to show and express it would have worked more in her favour than her 'kick ass' approach.

When I ask women what confidence means to them their responses are pretty similar and include:

- 'to be my authentic self',
- 'belief in myself and abilities',
- 'feeling good about myself',
- 'being able to do what I want',
- 'the ability to deal with anything that comes my way personally and professionally',
- 'to REALLY feel comfortable – not fake it'.

Self-help gurus often advocate 'faking it to you make it' but I think that advice should come with a warning. Don't get me wrong. Affirmations and modelling the behaviour of someone who has what you want can be effective in helping you acquire the mindset necessary to attract that skill or quality into your life, but only if you really believe what you are telling yourself is possible for you.

We'll do some work on beliefs and affirmations later in this book but right now just be aware that simply saying something doesn't necessarily make it true or happen. Very often we have behavioural patterns that are so ingrained and powerful that at a very basic level contradict the words we are mouthing.

Energetically speaking you won't feel comfortable or be congruent with your words and that will come across loud and clear, not only to others, but also more importantly to yourself. You'll feel like a fraud as your fear of being found out feeds a spiral of self-doubt, which in turn reduces your self-esteem and locks you in to a place where your confidence lags behinds your competence. This gap is not just one of fear or even procrastination but one of self-destruction; lost to yourself and the life you are meant to live.

As Within, So Without

There is a saying 'As Within, So Without'. This is a summary of the spiritual Law of Reflection, which states that our outside world is an exact reflection of our inner world. The Universe mirrors and reflects back to us all the good and bad, positives and negatives within ourselves and our lives.

If you doubt your ability or don't value your skills and talents, you will attract people who will steal your ideas, take credit for your work, play hardball and slash your fees. If you are self-critical and constantly beating yourself up with your thoughts, you will attract people who will reflect this by putting you down with verbal, psychological and possibly physical abuse. If you don't love and respect yourself, how can you expect that from others?

Authentic Confidence

We know authentic confidence when we see it. There is something about the person that tells us they are very comfortable with who they are. They know, like and trust themselves. Their essence is one of ease and positive expectation, trusting that they can handle whatever life throws at them. They operate from a place of faith rather than fear, because they understand themselves and are open to understanding and appreciating the perspective of others without feeling threatened or the need to be right.

In my mind the foundations of authentic confidence are contained within what I call the 3 C's of confidence – Clarity, Communication and Courage.

Clarity

When you are clear about who you are and what you value, what you want to give back to life or give life to; your purpose, a passion or a project, then attracting it into your life becomes so much easier. Clear thinking affords you the ability to be decisive, communicate your message accurately and enables others to respond accordingly.

Communication

When you are able to communicate clearly in a way that respects and honours you and others, when you have the courage to trust your innate wisdom, to follow your convictions and take action, which moves you from a feeling of being lost and stuck to one of freedom, and fulfilment, that's authentic confidence.

Courage

With authentic confidence you no longer give your power away by pleasing and appeasing other people. Your value and self-worth isn't wrapped up in others opinions of you, so you no longer feel the need to sacrifice yourself or seek others approval or permission to be, do and have what you want. You may seek advice and guidance but you don't act on it until you check within to ensure the advised action feels right with and for you.

When you hear that inner wisdom you will be ready to take the first small step forward. Authentic confidence doesn't mean that you won't feel fear about taking that step but what it does mean is that you have enough trust in yourself to face any challenge that initial step may present and remember it's the doing, the action that builds competence.

With authentic confidence you are free to be you, happy with yourself and by yourself if you so desire. Your masculine and feminine aspects are in balance, so that you can be strong without being threatening or aggressive and vulnerable without being or appearing weak. And, because you are being your authentic self, your attraction factor increases and you draw to you all the resources, support and nurturing you need. Your inner integrity is matched by those around you. As you begin to feel safe, secure, loved and happy on the inside, you learn to trust yourself, and the universe reflects this by surrounding you with people who love and support you and are as honest and generous as you are. As within, so without.

The 9 Elements of Authentic Confidence woven through the chapters of this book are:

Awareness
Understanding
Truth
Honour
Energy
Nurturing
Trust
Intuition
Commitment

Authentic confidence requires self-awareness, to become conscious of the inner game that thoughts play and the impact they have on our emotions and performance. It also requires you to understand how the people and events in your past and present have shaped and influenced you and why you may have to let some of these go to allow you to have the future you want.

You understand and appreciate it is 'how' you are being rather than 'who' you are being that will determine the quality of your life. Authentic confidence allows you to be true to yourself and honest with yourself about yourself, the good, the bad and the ugly and accepting that you are loveable and OK in spite of it. You honour yourself by living by your values and standing by your boundaries, being responsible and recognising how cause and effect plays out in your life. For every action there is a reaction or consequence.

You notice, and come to know, that everything in life consists of energy and has a vibration. I first became aware of this when I was teaching. Whenever I was tired or stressed I found the pupils challenging and badly behaved. Whenever I was energetic and happy I had fun learning and teaching. Fear is a heavy vibration, a lack of self-worth comes from negative self-talk which emits a low vibration and as we now know this combination will attract situations, individuals and circumstances of a similarly low vibration. On the other hand, self-worth and confidence radiate a high vibration and attracts people, situations and opportunities that match it. Knowing how to nurture oneself and the importance of consistently doing it, is key to developing authentic confidence, especially in moments of crisis. Never forget that we teach people how to treat us and by respecting ourselves and by caring for our mind, body and spirit we teach others to treat us well too.

Often called 'intuition', or the inner voice of feminine wisdom, call it what you will, but with authentic confidence you listen to it and in my experience it never fails to guide you to the correct path. And finally authentic confidence enables a commitment to self. It allows you to know that you deserve to have, to be and to do what you want and to be committed to doing whatever it takes to get there one small step at a time.

Now that may sound scary and a lot of hard work is needed to get you to that authentic place. All you have to do right now is believe in my belief in you. I encourage you to stay committed to your development and remember that you reap what you sow. I've been where you are now and have been seduced by promises of instant confidence but it's never lasted. What I will say is that you owe it to yourself to invest in yourself. You are worth the time and effort.

Lance Armstrong the famous cyclist and seven times winner of the Tour de France said, "You can't fake confidence, you have to earn it, you have to do the work."

You and I both know folk fake confidence all the time but what I do know is you can't fake authentic confidence because it takes a depth of self-knowledge, self-acceptance and self-worth that can't be faked and the great thing about authentic confidence is that it never feels like you've earned it but rather that you've rediscovered it because it's been there, within, all the time.

An Overview of the Confident You

We don't lack confidence in everything; we lack confidence in specific activities, within specific areas of life. The following exercise will provide an opportunity for you to consider the level of confidence you currently have in different areas of your life. It will provide you with the necessary focus and information for the rest of the activities in the book and provide an excellent opportunity for you to reflect on and review the current state of play in each area as well as how you would like each area to look in the future. You might also like to consider what kind of beliefs and thoughts you hold about you in those areas where your confidence is high and compare them to those you hold in areas where your confidence is low.

Exercise

The Wheel of Confidence on the next page consists of sections representing the broad areas of your life. I invite you to look at each of the sections and rate your level of confidence in each area on a scale of 1 to 10.

A rating of '1' represents low levels of confidence within this area of your life, it's likely you are very unhappy with the way things are in this area too.

A '10' represents a very high level of confidence and you are most likely to be totally content with this area of your life.

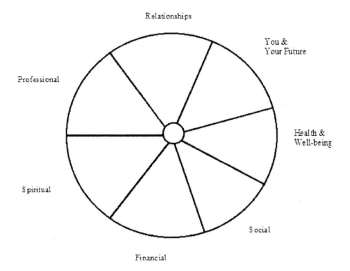

Before you begin to allocate a rating you might like to consider some of the questions I offer for your reflection for each area

Health & Wellbeing: Things to consider in this area are your physical fitness: exercise regime, diet, energy and stress levels.

- What kind of shape are you in both physically and mentally?
- Are you strong and healthy or could you be looking after yourself better?

Relationships: This section refers to your personal relationships with family, friends and significant others, I suggest you consider each separately as it will be a good source of information for future exercises.

- Do you feel comfortable enough to be yourself in this relationship? Do you feel loved and supported?
- Are you able to ask for what you want and need without fear of rejection or a critical response?
- Do you feel visible and heard?

Social: Is your social life how you would like it to be?

- Do you see friends often enough?
- Do you participate in a range of social events or do you do the same thing most of the time because it's comfortable?
- Do you have the confidence to go out or do you tend to socialise at home?
- Do you feel confident enough to meet new people and make new friends?
- How do you feel about talking to strangers, do you strike up conversations easily?

Professional: How confident do you feel at work?

- Are you able to speak out and share your views?
- Are you able to delegate or say 'No' when workload becomes overwhelming?
- Does your work fulfil you?

Financial: This section isn't about how much money you have, because your financial worth will never be enough unless your sense of self-worth is sufficient.

This section is more about your ability to manage your finances and provide for yourself and your family.

- Consider things like debts and savings and your management of them.

Spiritual: I've used the term spiritual here to refer to having a sense of purpose, meaning and direction in life, which helps contribute to the wider world.
This could be through your

- job
- community
- faith/religion
- environmental or charitable organisations

You: I believe that for something to change at a fundamental level in any area of your life, that change has to happen from the inside out and the 'You' section reflects your confidence in yourself and your future.

Self-confidence is the confidence within that I refer to as

- a felt sense of trust in yourself.
- your ability to get through whatever life throws at you even when you've been shocked and rocked at the very core of who you are.

Take time with each area and reflect on the questions before allocating a number between 1 and 10. The first number to come to mind is likely to be a most accurate reflection of how you really feel about this area of your life, but it's ok to sit with the number to get a sense of its accuracy. Remember confidence is a feeling, you'll know if this number feels right for you. Start with any area now and work your way round the circle.

Once you've given each area a mark out of ten, consider the following questions:

Why have you given yourself that score?

_____

_____

_____

_____

_____

What good stuff is currently going on in this area?

_____

_____

_____

_____

What could you do to improve things in this area of your life?

_____

_____

_____

_____

_____

What do you need right now to be happy with this area?

_____

_____

_____

_____

_____

Take an overview of your circle now.

- What stands out for you?

- What similarities do you see?

- Can you make any connections between the area's? E.g. similar beliefs, thoughts, attitudes, behaviours or influences.

- How might one area be impacting another?

- Who are the people who influence this area of your life? What thoughts/beliefs do they hold?

Make a note of these now:

Health and Well-being:

_____

_____

_____

_____

_____

Relationships: (Remember to consider, family, friends, significant other separately)

_____

_____

_____

_____

_____

_____

_____

_____

_____

_____

_____

Social:

_____

_____

_____

_____

_____

_____

Professional:

_____

_____

_____

_____

_____

Financial:

_____

_____

_____

_____

_____

Spiritual:

_____

_____

_____

_____

_____

You & Your Future:

_____

_____

_____

_____

_____

Hopefully by completing this exercise, and using the above questions to review your findings, you will have gained greater insight into your confidence levels and what strategies you use to support this confidence. For example you may feel very confident in the area of finance because you use a budget, have a regular saving plan etc. Your social confidence might be high because you always present yourself well, have a couple of topics to chat about and know to ask open questions.

Now that you have a good overview of where you are now in terms of confidence it's time to move on and we'll do that by taking a few steps back and considering who or what happened to affect your confidence but before we take a step back in time. Let's summarise what we know so far...

Confidence is

- Complex – you can be competent yet lack confidence which affects others belief in your ability. Arrogance, aloofness and other poor attitudes and behaviour are often a cover up job for a lack of confidence. Over confidence when lacking in competence has it's consequences.

- Fragile, influenced and impacted by people and events.

- Founded in clarity of thought, clear communication and the courage to take action and do what scares.

- Authentic confidence is deeply rooted in self-awareness, self-knowledge, self-acceptance, self-belief and a strong connection to your intuition.

Chapter 2 - Unpacking the Baggage

'If you are willing to deal with the past you can make the moment you are in rich'.

Oprah Winfery

We are products of our past. It is part of who we are today because whether you recognise it yet or not we use the patterns of the past in our daily lives.

What do I mean by patterns?

Well, I am referring to those helpful and sometimes unhelpful, beliefs and behaviours that we employ sometimes consciously, sometimes unconsciously in response to the behaviour of others and situations in which we find ourselves.

Our patterns are simply learnings from our past based on what we saw, heard and experienced from family, friends, teachers, colleagues, bosses, partners and anyone else who influenced us. It's also behaviour that generally worked for us on some level in terms of getting us the results we wanted or protecting us from a result we didn't want.

The problem we face is that our patterns can become destructive when they don't give us the results we want, since we employ them automatically. If we wish to grow in authentic confidence we have to pause, reflect and uncover the recurring themes that keep popping up in our life and the underlying lessons to be learned from them. Once you recognise a theme and get the learning behind it you can stop that pattern and create a new more helpful pattern, but for this to happen you have to become more self-aware, aware of how you give your power away through automatic reactions and self-sabotaging behaviour, which can often undermine your confidence.

Our past can't be changed but it can be used to inform our future and that's why it's important to spend some time with the pain from our past. Recognising and naming the patterns; the life/death/life cycles that run through our lives, exploring our feelings, examining guilt and being accountable for our role in the way events in our lives have played out is all part of the process.

What do I mean by being accountable?

Well, when something happens in our life that affects our confidence it helps to look at our reaction to the situation or circumstances. Have we chosen to play the helpless victim and dwell in our despair or did we respond by taking appropriate action? By reflecting on and reviewing our patterns of response we can become aware of our personal accountability for employing a victim mindset and our responsibility also to find alternative responses that will serve us better in the future and allow us to step up and in to our power.

Awareness is the first step in healing or changing, unpacking the baggage from our past so that we can understand it and make friends with it. Awareness will lighten its load and liberate us from the chains of pain so that it no longer affects but informs our future.

The work you will do in this chapter will require strength. It will require you to dig deep in to the wounds within so that they can heal. It will also require you to step up to the plate, to hold yourself responsible for giving your power away. It is important that you take your time with this chapter and nurture yourself whilst doing this work.

'Stuff' is likely to come up for you. Some of it you may have been unaware of before or if you had awareness it could be that you were unable to acknowledge just how damaging its impact has been. You might be shocked, deeply hurt, angered and tempted to beat yourself up further for your naivety or stupidity. STOP those thoughts! There is nothing to be gained from criticising or punishing yourself for something that happened in the past. You know from experience that your inner critic only diminishes your self-confidence. Releasing resentment and guilt through forgiving yourself and others is the only way forward.

I appreciate this is not an easy task, you may not know how to forgive, you may not even want to forgive.

I'll let you into a little secret. Forgiveness is a big challenge for me too, but if you are willing to forgive then you can start to heal. Let's get clear here on what forgiveness actually is. It is not about condoning events or behaviour. It's about being willing to let go and acknowledging that the perpetrator of your pain whether it be yourself or another was only working with what they knew at the time because that's where they were on their journey of personal growth.

Be gentle with yourself. I ask you to love, show compassion to your inner child for deep down it is she that is hurting, and it is she who will heal and help you rediscover your feminine wisdom and confidence within.

When you accept that you were doing the best you could with the knowledge and awareness you had at the time, self-love and authentic confidence begins to blossom.

By self-love I'm not referring to vanity or arrogance but referring to a gratitude and respect for yourself as a whole; mind, body and spirit. Self-love is expressed in our self-worth, which shows a deep appreciation for our gifts, skills and talents and an expectation of the same level of respect for our blessings from others.

Let's start the discovery and recovery process…

The following exercise will help with the first three elements of authentic confidence **Awareness, Understanding and Truth**. You will need to set some time aside for this exercise and I recommend you set yourself up in a quiet and comfortable environment and give yourself some uninterrupted time to complete it. You will also need a number of sheets of paper and maybe even some tissues because this work may cause a tear or two. Remember though there is power in tears, they provide healing, a route to new way of seeing and a new way of being.

Go back to the wheel of confidence and look at it again. Work your way round the circle starting with the area with the lowest confidence rating and complete the following exercise:

Exercise

For each area think through the various stages of your life you might want to consider it in blocks of time such as 5, 7 or 10 years. Think of times when you have experienced a lack of self-esteem or self-worth, where your confidence has been challenged or even been in crisis.

Describe these situations in as much detail as you can. *Who exactly was involved, what was said, was anyone else there, where did the event take place?* Capture as much emotion as you can. I invite you to also reflect on how you were feeling about yourself at that time.

Look for recurring themes e.g. allowing someone to take credit for your work, allowing issues to linger rather than addressing them right away, ignoring your intuition and following the advice of others.

Look for recurring patterns in how you have responded in these circumstances.

Health and Well-being:

_____

_____

_____

_____

_____

_____

_____

Relationships: (Remember to consider, family, friends, significant other separately)

_____

_____

_____

_____

_____

_____

_____

_____

_____

_____

_____

_____

_____

Social:

_____

_____

_____

_____

_____

_____

_____

Professional:

_____

_____

_____

_____

_____

_____

_____

Financial:

_____

_____

_____

_____

_____

_____

Spiritual:

_____

_____

_____

_____

_____

On completing this exercise what stands out for you?

_____

_____

_____

_____

_____

_____

_____

How are you feeling about what you've discovered?

_____

_____

_____

_____

_____

_____

What have you learned about yourself and your patterns of reaction?

_____

_____

_____

_____

_____

_____

Telling the Truth

Now we come to the healing heart of the matter, the third element of authentic confidence **Truth.** This will require courage and integrity as I invite you to tell the truth about yourself to yourself, for in doing so you no longer remain a victim haunted by the memories or scars of the confidence slumps you have experienced in the past or even today. You will be empowered by the knowledge and acknowledgement of the role you played in attracting those situations and people to you. You will take ownership of your deep and true feelings about yourself rather than listen to and be held back by the opinions of others. For their thoughts of you, are only thoughts and only true of you if you believe them to be.

On reviewing each of the events or circumstances that have had a negative impact on your confidence I invite you to reflect on how you were feeling about yourself at the time.

- Did you consider yourself not good enough?
- Perhaps you considered yourself less than, the people and the circumstances surrounding you?
- Might your ego be responsible for attracting a challenge to your confidence?

I want you to identify how in each situation you might be responsible for the result.

It might be something you did, it might be something you failed to do, or the way you set yourself up for the result e.g. failing to see the warning signs or choosing not to believe what you were seeing or hearing.

Perhaps you were guilty of ignoring your inner voice and listening to another's opinion because they spoke with authority whilst you courted self-doubt.

Consider the above questions in relation to past events now.

Taking stock of our past, acknowledging who or what affected our confidence is important because it allows us to engage with any emotions that arise, to express them rather than suppress them. By doing so we can let go of the pain forever yet treasure the nuggets of wisdom it affords us.

There is always value in the events or relationships that caused pain. If you allow yourself to uncover it, you will learn a great deal about yourself and come to realise how strong and powerful you really are. You learn lots about the other person too and what you've learned you can take forward in to the next relationship or similar situation that presents itself.

To allow the past to become the foundations for our future and be free of its pain requires a willingness to release emotions such as hurt, blame, anger and resentment and a willingness to forgive.

Some people may believe or perceive forgiveness as a sign of weakness but forgiveness of ourselves and others frees us from our past and allows us to live more consciously in the present. It is a path to peace. Spiritual Teachers often tell us that forgiveness and love is the answer to everything and whilst you might recognise and accept the truth of this, embracing the act of forgiveness can be more challenging.

Forgiveness can be used to take the moral high ground - to be better than an enemy or wrongdoer. True forgiveness is that of 'forgiving and forgetting', it is to remove all emotional attachment to a wrong that has been done to you, to let go of the memory and the hurt as if it never occurred.

The need to be right can be a huge obstacle to forgiveness. Being right can give one a sense of security, but the 'need' to be right is destructive to relationships and often masks feelings of insecurity. True forgiveness is about giving up the need to be right or wrong - all the time.

The need for revenge or the desire to cut people off and out of our lives, whilst resentment brews and stews, is easier initially but can lead to loneliness and disease until our hurt or anger fades. It can be much more helpful to sit with those feelings accepting that it's ok to feel what you feel, because they are a reaction to a violation of one of your values. It is this acceptance, which facilitates the letting go process.

Learning to Let Go

There are many ways to let go and I'll share a few with you here, which I have found particularly useful, but first you have to be willing to release. The following sequence of actions will help you discover how willing you really are.

- List all the things and even people you are willing to let go of.
- Then rate on a scale of 1-10 how willing you are to do this (With 1 representing not willing and 10 ready to let go).
- Notice your reactions.
- What are you willing to do to let these things or people go?
- How willing are you to do this (use the scale 1-10 to give you an indication)?
- What is your level of resistance?

Coming to a Place of Understanding

When it comes to negative thinking or feelings we can often want to put them away or deal with them quickly, the difficulty with this reactive approach is that we don't get to the root of the issue so we deny ourselves a depth of wisdom on how these negative experiences contribute to our lives.

Responding to our feelings facilitates an appreciative enquiry for what's going on within and around us. Through meditation or a journal we can make purposeful enquires about how a feeling came, what it's doing here and what it is about. Dialoguing with our negative emotions such as fear can help us to develop a healthy sense of caution, listening to our anger and addressing it dissolves frustration and develops a passion for life we might have missed had we not looked for the lesson. When we understand our unhelpful thoughts and feelings we refrain from resisting and are ready to release.

Physical Releasing

If the negative energy from experiences and emotions are not expressed they stay within where they can do varying degrees of harm. Take the emotion of anger it gets a lot of bad press in terms of emotions and has become a bit of a taboo. Yet there is nothing wrong with anger, it's a perfectly natural and acceptable emotion it's how it is expressed that can cause concern, if it's not given a safe voice it will find it's way to express itself in a torrent of rage at an inappropriate time or in the body through cuts and burns, burning sensations, boils and inflammation. Louise Hay's '*You Can Heal Your Life*' and Debbie Shapiro's '*Your Body Speaks Your Mind*' are excellent books for helping to understand how emotions link to illness or imbalances in the body.

I have found the following ways to physically release experiences and emotions really helpful.

Give yourself permission to get in touch with your pain and allow the tears to flow. I used to be quite challenged by this I guess because I believed tears were a sign of weakness and 'big girls don't cry' – well they do and they should and I knew that intellectually, but emotionally, I needed another excuse for it so I'd watch the film *Stepmom*, which is about the relationship between an x-wife and her two children and their coming to terms with the new wife. Julia Roberts is the step mom and Susan Sarridan the natural mother of two children who is dying of cancer and coming to terms with bequeathing the care of her children to a women she doesn't much care for. I think it's impossible to watch this film and not cry - it acted like a bit of a tap for me, which I could turn on and let the tears flow. If you struggle with letting the tears flow give this exercise a go of course the film doesn't need to be *Stepmom* but it does have to be a good tearjerker.

If the emotion is anger – a good scream in the car with the windows rolled up of course is a great way to release, as is punching into some pillows or, if you like the gym, a boxercise class is great too. Personally, I find going for a run works for me but I think any exercise that expends the excess adrenaline coursing through the veins will be beneficial.

Resentment is anger that is prolonged and continues well beyond the initial experience. When we are resentful, we are full of blame and we don't take responsibility, we take on the need for us to be right and someone else to be wrong. By releasing this need we take back our power to effect change, rather than being the victim of others cruelty. As long as you are angry at a situation or a person, that person or situation has power over you.

A good first step in the process of forgiveness is to try and gain some insight in to the other person's motives for behaving the way they did. The following exercise is an incredibly effective way of doing this. When you step into someone else's shoes, you feel like you have a better sense of them.

Exercise

Set out three different spaces on the floor, numbered 1 to 3. Each will have a different function and afford you a different perspective.

- In the first position, you will be looking out through your own eyes.
- In position two you will be the other party stepping into their shoes and imagining what it is like for them (this can be 1 person or a group it works the same).
- The third position involves taking an independent view, you get to step back and have a look at the two parties more dispassionately.

Choose a relationship you would like to explore.

- Stand in position 1 and imagine looking at the other person. Ask yourself, "What am I experiencing? What am I thinking? Feeling? etc. as I look at this person?"

  Ask any questions you might have for the person you've put in position 2

  Shake that position off!

- Go to position 2, imagine you are that person looking back at you in the first position. And ask yourself again, "What am I experiencing? What am I thinking? Feeling? etc. as I look at this person?"

Answer any questions that's been asked of you.

Shake that position off!

- Move to the third position, looking at both people in the situation and ask yourself, "What am I experiencing? What am I thinking? Feeling?" As you look at the person in the first position what do you see?

Think about how your thoughts and feelings compared in all thee positions.

- Go back and revisit the second position. Ask yourself, "How is it different now, what has changed?" Finish by coming back to first position and ask yourself, "How is this different now, what has changed?"

Now that you've gained an insight into why the other person behaved the way they did, you are more able to forgive and let go so now.

- Imagine the person sitting in front of you. Say to that person, "I forgive you for ..." and imagine good things happening to that person. Say to that person, "May life's richest blessings be yours."

  You may find this difficult to do, but keep doing it until you have released the resentment.

  Now turn your attention to yourself and say out loud "I forgive myself for ....." and keep doing it until you feel lighter.

Energetic Releasing

You can have anything you wish for in your life but if your happiness and sense of self-worth **depend** on having it, then you are attached to it through energetic cords. Negative energies such as pride, envy, need and greed can send huge cords to things and objects such as houses, cars, money and jobs.

I got a pretty hefty lesson on The Spiritual Law of Attachment when I got made redundant. Then, I was a material girl all caught up in my designation and what my money could buy me and where it could take me on holiday. I was all caught up in the so-called 'trappings of wealth'.

Now there is nothing wrong with having money and having nice things but what I discovered was that when I lost my job not only did I lose the trappings of wealth, I lost my sense of identity with it. The attachment to these things kicked off my confidence crisis when I lost them, but this loss became a find when I realised that it was the same event that help me rediscover my authentic confidence independent of status, finance or emotional need.

Cords are formed between people who have unresolved issues between them too. The Law of Attachment teaches that, whoever or whatever, you are attached to can control and manipulate you. Every time you send thoughts or words of anger, envy or jealousy to someone, you manifest a thread, which attaches to them. You can also attach yourself to someone through a need for their love or recognition. An occasional positive thought may dissolve it, but if you consistently send out negative feelings, the threads will form cords. These will remain and bind you together, until they are released.

The following exercise will help you to the cut the cords and move on. You will need some notepaper, a pen, a white candle, some red ribbon, a safety pin, a pair of scissors and a photo of the person you wish to be released from.

Read the instructions through a couple of times before you complete it. Set aside a couple of hours for this and again set yourself up in quiet environment where you will not be disturbed.

Exercise

When you are ready light the candle and begin by writing down all the things that the other person did or said that hurt you. Now you will cry, you make get angry and punch a cushion or two, you may even throw in a little swearing but that's OK, better out than in, get it all down on paper. When you are feeling there's nothing left to write just pause, take a deep breath in, then start to think about the good things this person brought into your life, the times you laughed, the gifts they gave, all the good stuff, write it down and give thanks for it.

When you've finished place their photo in the paper, roll the paper up and tie it with the red ribbon. Make sure that there is enough ribbon hanging from the scroll for you to attach it to yourself with the pin.

Holding the scroll in one hand and the scissors in the other, say the following:

'Dear ...

I forgive you for all the pain you have caused and ask that you forgive me too.

I thank you for all gifts of insight and learning you gave me.

I now release you with love.'

Cut the red ribbon tied between yourself and the scroll and burn the scroll wrapped in its ribbon. If you wish you may keep the ribbon and pin attached to you as a keepsake of the purification and release of your relationship or just burn that too.

All of the exercises I've shared in this chapter are cleansing and powerful but you may find that some experiences are easy to let go of whilst others linger, so do these exercises regularly until you find your anger and resentment has dissolved.

Now that you have unpacked the baggage from the past and hopefully cleared some of it, we are ready to move forward into the present and look at your belief system but before we do let's summarise what's been covered so far.

Summary

- Our past can't be changed but it can be used to inform our future.

- If we wish to grow in authentic confidence, we have to pause and reflect and uncover the recurring themes that keep popping up in our life and the underlying lessons to be learned from them. Once you recognise the theme and learn from it you can stop that pattern, create and learn a new, more helpful pattern.

- Forgiveness isn't about condoning what happened it's about acknowledging it, seeing past it, being willing to let go of the pain it caused and move on. The word forgive means to 'give for' you are giving for the purpose of being free.

- Authentic Confidence requires for you to tell the truth to yourself about yourself.

- If the negative energy from experiences and emotions are not expressed they stay within where they can do varying degrees of harm but they can be released through physical and spiritual exercises to allow one to return to a state of health and well-being.

- Self-love is expressed in our self-worth, which shows a deep appreciation for our gifts, skills and talents and an expectation of the same level of respect for our blessings from others.

Chapter 3 - You're not the girl you think you are

'Choose beliefs that serve your soul - choose beliefs that serve the grander dream of who you choose to be'.

Joy Page

We humans are meaning makers. We can take any experience of our lives and create a meaning that either empowers us or holds us back. One woman's nightmare is another woman's dream. It really is a question of perspective and expectation, which then becomes a self-fulfilling prophecy as what you believe to be true of you becomes exactly so. You see we humans also need to be right, so we search for and accumulate evidence to prove our position.

The other evening I was out with some friends for a little celebration. One of my single friends declared to have lost all interest in men, claiming only to attract losers, idiots and drunkards, whilst refuting all disagreements to the contrary. As we were leaving the bar a drunk man passed and shouted across, "Hello ya big darlin!"

"See, see what I mean," she retorted.

Absolutely! You see that's exactly what she expected and that's what she attracted. Another friend is very confident in her attraction factor and is never without a dinner date. She expects the best and gets it and is often whisked off to some exotic resort with her current beau.

We form our beliefs as a result of our experiences and experiences are the result of our beliefs. I think it's important to be aware of how the brain manages our experiences because that awareness can help us consider whether the beliefs we hold help or hinder us. It is in this chapter we again consider the T of Authentic confidence looking for the truth within our beliefs and uncovering any lies they may hold within them.

How the brain manages our experiences

To prevent sensory overload we pay attention to certain dimensions of our experience and exclude others. What is deleted is out of our conscious awareness. Now this can be useful or not, depending on the application.

For example, when you are concentrating on a task in a busy office you can delete the noise surrounding you and focus on the task in hand. That's when deleting is useful. Sometimes it's not useful when you hear only criticisms and none of the compliments.

When Laura came to see me she was very down and stressed about her career in the Fire and Rescue service. She was concerned about feedback she had received about her performance and in particular her ability to work in a busy environment often being teased by her colleagues as 'zoning out'. When we looked over Laura's CV and her annual appraisal documentation we discovered that things were not as bleak as she had come to believe. Firstly, she had failed to acknowledge to herself that she was on a learning curve for a new career and wouldn't be expected to know it all. She had been in the fire service less than 2 years having previously spent 10 years in a library. When she recognised that the 'zoning out' was not day dreaming but pure concentration on getting paperwork completed in a noisy environment she was able to change her perception of this from a fault to a skill. When she focused on what had gone well during her working day she realised that her successes far out numbered what she perceived as failure. Instead of interpreting the things that hadn't gone so well as failure she began to see it as feedback which she used to propel her career forward.

We also distort what we see, hear and feel. Distortion is all about the meaning we make of our experience. We create meaning that helps or hinders, but seldom do we question the meaning we are making.

Have you ever caught someone looking at you and maybe smiling, and you start to get annoyed thinking, 'What are they looking at?' and thinking them really rude or laughing at you. Then when they pass you they give you a compliment like, "Love your shoes. Where did you get them?" Or have you ever heard someone say, "He never buys me flowers so he doesn't love me," but when challenged, that person could find a host of other examples which demonstrate how their partner loves them. For example, breakfast in bed, cleaning their car.

We also make sweeping statements and generalise an experience by applying it to a multitude of other situations just like my friend who always attracts losers and fails to count the really nice guys she has dated or find her attractive.

Beliefs are ideas that you hold on to and deeply trust. They can be positive and empowering or negative and disempowering and they have a profound effect on our levels of self-confidence. Seldom do we question our beliefs because we hold them to be true at the core of our being. Authentic confidence allows us to uncover any lies within our beliefs by questioning and uncovering the truth behind what we believe about ourselves, others and the world, and examining the generalisations we make and the information we distort or delete.

Our confidence is challenged when we hold unhelpful beliefs around what is possible for us, our ability to achieve it and, perhaps most worryingly, whether we are worthy of it. It is not uncommon for these beliefs to come from the influence of what others have told us or their expectations of us e.g. the media, parents, teachers, colleagues, bosses and partners.

Let's say you had a couple of relationships that ended badly. You may come to believe that you are no good at relationships (generalisation). In fact, you may have been told this from an ex-partner which only serves to reinforce that belief. I'm sure however there were times when you were both happy and things were going well and the relationship was good (deletions). You have other relationships with friends, family and colleagues that are fulfilling.

By now you are getting the picture of how your thinking can be distorted. What I would suggest is that you don't currently have an effective and successful strategy for nurturing romantic relationships. Fortunately, this can be explored and developed until you are able to enjoy a fulfilling relationship. This is true of anything that you desire, which you currently believe is out of your reach. You will never achieve it until you challenge the limiting belief and change the can't do attitude to a CAN DO!

Exercise

If you are carrying the burden of a belief ingrained in you from someone in your past – a parent, teacher, partner - it's time to return the belief back to its source.

The following exercise will help you do this. It works equally well for emotions and secrets without you having to disclose them.

- Get very clear about what the belief is and the emotions related to it.
- Mentally put the belief in a box and wrap it up.
- Visualise the source of that belief – teacher, parent, sibling - standing in front of you.
- Greet them and then say out loud, "This belief does not serve me or belong to me and I give it back to you, its source."
- See in your mind's eye the person take the box.
- Then say, "Bless you, now bless off," and watch them and their belief box disappear.

Limiting beliefs are the major culprits that prevent us from achieving our aspirations and living the life we desire. Buried deep in our subconscious, they are often tied into our self-image and our perceptions of the world. On the plus side, they are self-protective and survival oriented. On the negative side, they act as rules that keep us from attaining the possible, restraining us from what we are capable of and what we deserve.

You see when a person states a limiting belief they are often focusing on what they don't want (limitation), rather than what they do want (outcome). Limiting beliefs can also sometimes confuse identity with behaviour. Unhelpful identity labels like 'I'm shy' or 'I'm a slow learner' imply that these are fixed qualities, rather than a combination of ideas, feelings and behaviours.

A few years back sales was a dirty word to me, I hated it. Rather than focusing on the sales I made my focus was on the rejections, which eventually developed into a limiting belief of 'I'm no good at sales'. When I explored this belief with my NLP training buddy Ben, a superb salesman, I had a belief busting moment.

I explained to Ben that I enjoyed meeting people and talking to them about how I could help them and how I worked but I always got really uncomfortable with what I saw as the 'here comes the sales bit'.

Ben and I explored things further, discussing how the belief 'I can't sell' served me and if it were true. Looking at the facts - I had a regular flow of consultancy and coaching work with repeat clients. I had a large list of subscribers to my newsletter and online community. I had a substantial database of subscribers to GROW, my networking business, with a good number of business owners attending each event. I began to see that the belief wasn't true, it was a lie – the evidence proved it. The belief was merely a protection racket, to save me from the rejection I feared.

If you hear yourself using words or hearing words like 'can't, should, shouldn't, could, couldn't, would, ought or ought not' chances are there is a limiting belief lurking around. Be aware of your language, because once you are aware of it you can do something about it.

Remember, beliefs are only true if you act as if they are. What you choose to believe becomes your reality so if a thought or a belief isn't serving you change it because YOU CAN!

Consider this...

At some point in your life you believed you couldn't have something or do something like riding a bike, swimming, driving, public speaking, or stopping smoking for example. Now at some point perhaps with practice you began to doubt this belief and change your mind about it until eventually you could do it.

Right?

Beliefs change through life and there is a natural process to this. We become dissatisfied with current circumstances, we begin to doubt the belief is true and want to believe something else and so we develop a new belief and let go of the old limiting belief.

The next exercise will help you uncover your limiting beliefs and change them to more empowering ones.

Exercise

- Write down the limiting belief you have, **Remember** they usually start with can't, should etc.

- Read the limiting belief out loud then listen to the inner dialogue that begins to play.

- Ask what past experience reinforces that belief.

- How might these experiences have led to your belief?

- Is this belief still valid?

- What evidence do I have to support this belief?

- Who do I know who holds an opposite belief?

- What evidence suggests that the belief is untrue?

- In what ways is the belief ridiculous?

Find an alternative belief

The universe abhors a vacuum so there is no point in getting rid of a limiting belief without finding an alternative to fill its place, so ask your-self, 'What would be a more empowering belief to hold?' The best way to do this is to brainstorm for possibilities. You may have to try a few on before you find one that's a good fit for you.

Make sure the new belief is stated in the positive and makes you feel good about yourself.

E.g. I am good at relationships, I can sell, I am a successful networker.

Integrate the new belief

Imagine how things will be different when you hold this new belief. What will you be doing and saying? How will you be feeling?

The key to the success of your belief change is becoming more aware of your *circle of influence*. Your circle of influence is the people from the past and present who have and do influence your belief systems. If a belief comes from your upbringing or educational background then this is what you've been taught to believe and is simply programming. The key question to ask your-self about these beliefs is, 'Does this still hold true for me today'?

As for the people presently in your life be mindful of how they treat you, listen carefully to how they talk to you and talk about you, as well as what they say about the world in general. How do their beliefs influence you? Do they have a positive impact on your self-confidence? Are they supportive? If not, remember you have a choice. You can tolerate or you can eliminate your confidence drainers; the thieves who steal your self-esteem and self-worth. You can do this by limiting your time with them or deciding they no longer deserve a place in your life. Don't be surprised if once you change your beliefs they seem to disappear from your life because energetically their power and influence over you has gone.

Summary

- We can take any experience of our lives and create a meaning that either empowers us or holds us back.

- We form our beliefs as a result of our experiences, but we only pay attention to certain dimensions of our experiences: to prevent sensory overload we delete and distort the information we receive as well as making generalizations that aren't always helpful.

- Our confidence is challenged when we hold unhelpful beliefs around what is possible for us, our ability to achieve it and perhaps most worryingly whether we are worthy of it.

- When a person states a limiting belief they are often focusing on what they don't want (limitation) rather than what they do want (outcome).

- Words such as can't, should, shouldn't, could, couldn't, would, ought or ought not, are often an indication that there is a limiting belief lurking about.

Chapter 4 – The Importance of Self-Honour

'To free us from the expectations of others, to give us back to ourselves – there lies the great, singular power of self-respect'.

Joan Didion

Self-honour is at the heart of authentic confidence and is about putting the right things in place so that self-care and self-confidence can flourish. Self-honour is about getting to the very essence of your being and learning to love and respect the woman you are. It's about letting go of faulty thinking, which creates feelings of not being good enough, and releasing from your life self-sacrificing patterns and even people that drain you, so that you can become free from the tolerations and exploitations that hold you back.

Self-Honour allows you to release yourself from the lady in waiting routine and step up and into your power so that you no longer remain a victim of circumstance, but become victorious in living a happy and prosperous life. The work you have completed in previous chapters will have revealed the recurring themes in your life that have dented your confidence and self-esteem. You'll have become aware of the beliefs and perhaps patterns of behaviour that limit you. Now is the time for you to relearn the art of giving and receiving so that you can give without giving up yourself, regain a better perspective of your skills and talents and learn to trust your inner wisdom rather than seek someone else's approval or validation. In order to do that you have to become aware of what you are currently putting up with.

Tolerations

If you think about it, we are raised to tolerate a lot of things in life we don't like. How often have you heard:

- "Life's Hard."
- "You can't have everything you want."
- "Don't complain."
- "Be grateful for what you do have."
- "Say nothing, best not to rock the boat.
- "Don't be selfish."

Tolerations often represent compromises you have been talked into or talked yourself into. They can also come from behaviour patterns we've unconsciously modelled from others, in particular, our mothers.

I'm not having a go at mothers here but as nurturers they often demonstrate self-sacrificing behaviours that we then employ without realising. This then leads to seeing to everyone's needs first and forgetting about your own. Consider this - who normally takes the dodgy looking prawn cocktail at Christmas with the attitude 'That one will do me'? Whilst this example is simplistic, it strikes a punch when you consider that women play it out on a daily basis.

Self-sacrificing behaviour can make you feel noble and virtuous but can become a vice with a destructive impact on your self-esteem, because when you put yourself last most of the time you are unconsciously sending a message to yourself and to others that you're not worthy.

There are other things that you might be tolerating that could be affecting your confidence, dampening your spirits and draining your energy. Perhaps a colleague doesn't give you the respect you desire; keeps you waiting before a meeting or allows unnecessary and lengthy interruptions during meetings. Perhaps something in your home needs repair or a room needs redecorated so that it feels more comfortable. Perhaps you are tolerating being in debt or not charging/earning enough for the work that you do.

When Celine came to see me, she was feeling very lost and confused. Stuck in a 'dead-end job' way beneath her skill level, Celine was earning a lot less than she was used to and incurring mounting debt accompanied by feelings of guilt and shame. She was mourning the woman she once was and the life she had, before moving from Quebec to Glasgow to be with her boyfriend.

To help Celine move forward we identified that addressing her debt issues would make the biggest difference to her confidence. We reframed her view of debt so that she could see it as a tool that had helped her to keep everything in flow and allow her to live a decent lifestyle. That way rather than beating herself up about it she could see it had served its purpose - giving her the freedom and ability to enjoy life. We then developed an action plan to increase the inflow and decrease the outflow of cash. She sold items on eBay, at car boot sales, swapped credit cards to get better interest rates and devised a budget. Within weeks her activity had made quite an impact on her debt and her confidence.

We worked on her CV, identifying her network and clarifying her personal brand. It was at this point

Celine admitted to herself that it was her relationship that wasn't working any more. She and her partner were no longer compatible, their values and aspirations were different, she was working hard to reduce debt while he was creating more. She wanted to move to a smaller house, he wanted to stay where he was. Celine recognised and reconciled with the fact that she had been tolerating the debt and the dead-end job as a way to avoid ending a relationship that deep down she knew wasn't working.

I bet that whatever you are tolerating doesn't make you feel good but what you must recognise and accept is that on some level it's working for you otherwise the toleration wouldn't exist.

For example, it may be helping you temporarily to avoid making a decision that will cause you some pain or unhappiness, or it may be a fear of what might happen if you assert yourself. Remember this, when you tolerate you become less attractive to yourself and to others and you have less impact, which in turn can often lead to you being crippled by feelings of helplessness and hopelessness.

You may be reading this and think you are not tolerating anything. Well if that's true good for you. However, if you are justifying why a certain area of your life is the way it is then the chances are you ARE tolerating something and I would invite you to reconsider.

Try the following exercise to get clear on and clear of your tolerations. It's important that you write these down so that you can actually see them rather than just thinking about them. Write down the tolerations that seem impossible to solve as it's likely that smaller tolerations stem from these.

Exercise - Getting Clear On and Clear of Tolerations

- For each of the following categories write down a list of at least ten tolerations:

Car.

Equipment.

Home.

Office.

Work.

Relationships - family, friends, significant other, colleagues. Consider their behaviour, habits, attitude and communication style.

You - Your habits, behaviour, attitudes and communication style, health and well-being.

- Beside the tolerations write down how these are serving you. What benefits are you perceiving from putting up with the situation?

- What are these tolerations costing you?
  These can be measured in terms of time, resources and money or the opportunity cost, level of attraction e.g. respect, recognition. Remember these are likely to impact more on your confidence.

- Commit to eliminating the tolerations from your list.

To be toleration free means that you don't put up with negative situations or behaviours from other people. The benefit of this is that you'll have more energy, be happier and feel more confident because you have clear boundaries.

Setting Healthy boundaries

Boundaries are critical to self-care and essential for self-confidence. They allow you to be clear about what's important to you, they help you to teach others how to treat you and they facilitate a way for you to balance meeting your needs with the needs of others.

Start with the small stuff

If you are not used to drawing boundaries, it can be a bit of a challenge. I would advise that you start small.

For example, if you have to be up early for work you might decide to make it a personal rule not to take or make telephone calls after 9pm. By letting friends and family know your decision they are unlikely to call and will only do so if it's urgent. Once you get comfortable with setting boundaries like this you will find it less of a challenge to draw a line when confronted with a bigger issue.

Express rather than suppress your needs

Know exactly what you want and be specific when you are asking for it but most importantly believe that it is possible for you to have it. The following is a good formula to go by:

- Say the person's name.
- Say what you want.
- Say why you want it.
- Say when you want it.
- Say thank you rather than please as it assumes cooperation.

Remember to avoid blame and unnecessary upset state how you are feeling rather than what the other person is doing wrong. E.g. I feel my input isn't valued when arrangements are made without consulting me.

Remember you have a choice

When you are asked to do something, remember you can say yes or you can say no. You don't have to commit right away. Buy yourself some time and say, "Can I think about it and get back to you?" If you are pressurised for a response give a time and date, if necessary, as to when you will respond and during that time consider the following questions:

- What are my options?
- What do I want?
- What feels like the right thing for me to do in this situation?
- What am I sacrificing? Does it feel OK to sacrifice in this situation? Is it appropriate?
- What's most important to me right now?

Take a heart centered approach to decision making

When it comes to decision making get out of your head and as the song says 'Listen to your heart'. Go to a quiet place on your own and centre yourself by breathing deeply. Once you feel a deep sense of peace, you can ask yourself the following questions:

- What do I need to know before I make this decision?
- What's the best way for me to deal with this situation?
- What do I have to do now?

Be still and patient and trust the answers will arise.

Delegate

Do the tasks you enjoy and are good at and ditch those that don't play to your strengths. You can delegate these to someone who is better at them and this will free up your time and energy.

Become a top priority

Schedule regular 'me time' activities in to your day. Remember a little self-care gets you there. Giving more to yourself means that you are more able to give to others. Remember stress is a reaction to a block in the flow of giving and receiving and you can't give what you haven't got.

If you find yourself fearful of setting boundaries then you might need to do a bit of detective work to uncover what's stopping you. It might be that your need to be needed is allowing you to encourage over dependency and thus the payoff is the benefits that being a rescuer or a martyr brings. I invite you to consider what specifically these benefits are and what the possible costs and impact this behaviour is costing you and the other person both in the short term and the long term.

The Spiritual Law of Responsibility is about being able to respond appropriately to a person or situation and not take responsibility for them. When we make others decisions for them we don't serve their highest growth.

One of my clients, Lynne, came to me very stressed and depressed because of her relationship with her sister. Her sister who had enjoyed a great deal of success in the world of recruitment had embarked on a new career and was stuck in the confidence competence gap when it came to her new role and life style. Lynne felt her sister had become over dependant on her, fearful of making a decision without her input or approval. Rather than set clear boundaries, Lynne had tried to pull away completely and that only made the relationship more desperate; one woman fearful of losing the support and friendship of the sister she loved, the other fearful of her health and wellbeing as she was completely overwhelmed by her sister's neediness. As we worked together, Lynne came to realise that making her sister's decisions for her and allowing her sister to take up most of her time and energy had held her sister back from recognising her own strength and competence. For Lynne the payoff had been a prevention mechanism from stepping in to her purpose and passion due to a fear of being a successful business owner.

Another reason for failing to set boundaries is a fear of offending by saying NO. However, when you have clear boundaries it's easier for you to assert yourself because when a line has been crossed you have a better understanding of the emotional, mental and physical impact that certain situations or behaviours from others is likely to have on you. You are more aware of the reasons why this boundary is in place and more able to explain to yourself and others why crossing this line is not acceptable. This knowledge allows you to recognise when someone or something is teetering on the line because your inner guidance signals warnings and as always it's up to you to heed them. Remember also that not being able to tell someone something for fear of hurting them or making them jealous is taking responsibility for their feelings, which disempowers them, and a disempowered person is always an angry person.

When you are clear about your boundaries your self-trust, self-respect and authentic self-confidence glows for others to see. You are well aware of what you will accept and what you won't and that makes it easier for you to teach others how to treat you.

People like to know who they are dealing with and where they stand in a relationship whether it's personal or professional. We tend to live our lives by a set of rules and in a way that's what boundaries are. They help to instil a sense of trust and confidence as people get to know what they can expect from you and what you will accept from them, and that speaks volumes as to how much you value yourself. It reminds me of my teaching days. Being firm and fair in the classroom is rewarded with respect, effort and a good ethos and well they do say relationships are the curriculum of the school of life.

Summary

- Self-Honour is at the heart of authentic confidence. It is about putting the right things in place so that self-care and self-confidence can flourish.

- Tolerations often represent compromises you have been talked into or talked yourself into.

- Self-sacrificing behaviour can be virtuous but can also have a destructive impact on your self-esteem.

- Recognise that every toleration has a payoff for you.

- Having healthy boundaries is important for your self-worth and self-respect.

- Failure to set healthy boundaries can be tied up with a need to be needed, fear of offending, fear of failure or fear of success.

- Clear boundaries build trust and respect in others and in your-self.

- Your responsibility is to empower and strengthen others and encourage them to carry their own responsibilities, make their own decisions and their own way in life.

Chapter 5 – Self Care

'Love yourself first, and everything else falls in line. You really have to love yourself to get anything done in this world'.

Lucille Ball

Self-love is expressed through self-care and self-care allows authentic confidence to show and flow with an ease that is transparent for all to see. Self-care demonstrates that a person respects themselves and knows what they need to do, be and have to enjoy a happy, fulfilling and balanced personal and professional life.

Any change in confidence requires a change in attitude and behaviour, self-care requires you to be mindful of self-sabotaging beliefs and self-sacrificing behaviours, pausing to question them rather than allowing them to run on automatic pilot. You take time to ponder what your needs are and then focus on having them met.

You give up on reeling with resentment and disappointment when others don't meet your needs because you know they're not mind readers and you must ask for what you want. If you need help or support with a project or a shoulder to cry on, you allow yourself to let go of any dysfunctional independent behaviour and ask for support and you are open to receiving it when it's offered rather than play the martyr.

You let go of any assumptions or judgments about people's willingness to give because you recognise that one never knows what a person is capable of or willing to do until you ask them. Even if the first person you ask says 'No' you learn not to interpret it as a personal rejection but accept that they just don't have the support to give at the time and appreciate that they are in turn simply taking care of them self and so you are free to ask someone else.

With self-care, you let go of the good girl role, people pleasing pantomimes and the guilt of saying, "No," and, "Enough Already!" You know your boundaries and can stick to them or negotiate them depending on whether it might serve you or not. You become more aware of what I call the thieves and the big Ds in your life - the doubters and dimmers – people who doubt your ability, dim down your light, and steal your sparkle by playing down your success and making a big deal of small stuff that's gone wrong.

Then there are the dream stealers who try to talk you out of taking risks that they wouldn't dream of taking themselves for fear of failure or fear of you succeeding and leaving them behind.

Time thieves are people who for one reason or another take up more of your time and support than you have to give. To be fair, time thieves aren't always people. It might be work, or a particular activity that's becoming all consuming. Have you ever been on the web to check something out only to find that you've been sucked up in the surf and lost hours? Has it become a routine to stay late at the office to finish a task?

Then there are the mood thieves. You bump into these people feeling great and leave them feeling down. But perhaps the most dangerous of the pack, and the ones requiring the most courage to challenge, are the confidence thieves. Confidence thieves are often driven by envy and try to strip you of your self-esteem by their words or actions.

Being aware of both time and energy draining people and activities in your circle of influence and learning to limit your exposure to them is essential for good self-care.

Learning to nurture your-self, by spending time with people and activities that feed your soul builds energy and authentic confidence, and helps you to live a balanced and fulfilling life.

I know from experience that not moving and working my body leaves me feeling uptight and out of balance so every morning I start my day with yogalates; a combination of yoga and pilates moves to set me up for the day ahead. I'm not saying I always feel like it, especially if I have an early appointment, but what I will say is that I feel the difference when I don't do it. I've learned therefore to take a No Excuses approach to this daily self-care regime.

My other self-care practices include 'me time' coffee breaks where I go out for a coffee on my own and appreciate the soothing feelings a latte provides me. I love going for walks in my local park and to have fresh flowers around the house especially in my office. Natural beauty inspires me.

I'm not suggesting for a moment you live beyond your means. Self-care is about aiming to eliminate stress from your life and part of that is clearing any financial clouds that are looming over you. If you have done the work in the previous chapters you've come to recognise your tolerations and developed some boundaries to help eliminate the stresses and strains that are undermining your confidence. Now I want you to consider how you might nurture yourself to authentic confidence. If you are thinking that such activities are selfish I invite you to consider another perspective.

The Law of Responsibility will not allow you to take on great responsibility in life if you do not take care of your own needs. Your emotions and spirit need to be looked after, self-care is an investment in the health of your mind, body and spirit but more importantly your happiness. You're not being selfish you are being 'self full' and when you are 'self full' it is much easier to give without feelings of resentment or sacrificing your own wellbeing. You deserve to be the best possible version of yourself and doing things that make you feel good lifts your energy. As you reduce your obligations and minimise your commitments you might feel that you are doing less but you are probably being more productive. You become lighter, more fulfilled and fun and people become attracted to your positive vibe.

The following exercise will help you identify the things that feed your soul and find ways to put more of them into your life.

Exercise

Make a list of at least ten things you love to do that makes you feel great. You can include people you enjoy spending time with...

1

2

3

4

5

6

7

8

9

10

For each of the above ten items, think of three different ways to incorporate each in your life then identify which ones you could incorporate in to your daily life and do it now.

Learning to Listen

The I in authentic confidence stands for **Intuition** and it is here that I invite you to learn to listen to this inner wisdom that is often gently offered. Whilst we tend to think of only the special few having a sixth sense it is present in each and every one of us. It may present itself as a feeling, a gentle inner voice, a sense of knowing. You might refer to it as a gut reaction, your vibes, your instinct, whatever you choose to call it, learn to listen because it will always serve you well.

I am sure that you have had times when you knew that on some level something wasn't right for you and you proceeded with disastrous effects? Perhaps whilst looking for a new home you instantly knew which one was for you when you walked through the door – that's your sixth sense at play.

Sometimes we can be fully engaged in activities such as ironing or washing the dishes when inspiration or solutions to problems flow in. Being fully absorbed in doing something is a form of meditation and provides a gap for guidance to flow from our authentic self. Sometimes we have to make time to sit and listen by creating a space to let guidance flow through formal meditation, other times guidance comes as a reaction to what we are experiencing. When I feel something or someone isn't right for me my energy drops and I want to move away as soon as possible.

Learning to listen to your inner wisdom is just a matter of being mindful about what your body is trying to tell you, being aware of your feelings and operating from the heart rather than figuring things out in your head all the time. All you have to do is create peace and quiet and space just to be. I go to the park to do this. Other options might be to take a yoga or meditation class or go for a walk in the hills or on the beach. Connecting with nature is a great way to ease and feed the spirit.

Self-care isn't without its challenges from self and others. You may find yourself resisting to make the commitment to keep up your daily self-care practice and if work or family life becomes more demanding, it's easy to slip into the old routine of letting yourself slip further down in the priorities of your never ending to do list. You may even find yourself being accused of being selfish when you don't dance to the beat of other peoples drum.

My advice is to develop a thick skin against these accusations and become committed to taking care of yourself because when you fail to keep commitments you become less credible to yourself, your self-trust diminishes and so does your confidence. The good news is that every time we keep a commitment to ourselves we become more credible, we trust more and gain more confidence.

Summary

- You can't take on great responsibility in life if you don't take care of your own needs. When you take care of yourself first you are then in a fit state to help others.

- Self-care demonstrates that a person respects themselves and knows what they need to do, be and have to enjoy a happy, fulfilling and balanced personal and professional life

- Self-care is about being honest with yourself and others about what your needs are and focusing on having them met.

- Self-care is about giving yourself permission to ask for what you want, to seek help without feeling weak or needy, and saying no without feeling guilty. Self-care is your self-protection policy for good health and wellbeing.

- Learning to nurture your-self by spending time with people and activities that feed your soul builds energy and authentic confidence and helps you to live a balanced and fulfilling life.

- The mind, body, spirit is one system learning to listen to your intuition, being aware of your energy and your feelings which is feedback from the body are all key to self-care.

Chapter 6 – Developing your Confidence Resource Kit

'Confidence is preparation. Everything else is beyond your control'.

R Kline

I've said it before and I'll say it again. Confidence is like a pendulum swinging from one extreme to the other depending on what's going on your in your life, what you are doing and who you are with. Having your own confidence resource kit will help you know what to do when your confidence deserts you. This chapter contains tips tools and techniques for you to use on those occasions.

Confidence is an inside job and the first thing to develop in your confidence resource kit is your mindset.

What exactly is mindset?

Mindset was discovered by Stanford University psychologist Carol Dweck through decades of research on achievement and success. Dweck discovered that there are two mindsets a *fixed mindset* and a *growth mindset*. In a fixed mindset, people believe that their intelligence and talent are fixed traits and spend their time documenting these rather than developing them. They believe that success is due to effortless talent. Dweck says they are wrong.

In a growth mindset, people believe that their abilities can be developed through persistence, dedication and hard work. In their view, brains and talent are a starting point. If you read Napoleon Hill's book *Think and*

Grow Rich he points out that virtually all great people have had these qualities. They've been lifelong learners, patrons of the possibility virus and been persistent in the pursuit of their goals and in so doing built resilience and authentic confidence.

Now I appreciate your mindset at the moment may be flawed with doubt and scepticism about what is possible for you, but your doubts are products of habitual thinking not accurate thinking. It may be that you have reached a plateau on the learning curve and rather than give in and up I urge and advise you to develop patience and persistence. Take it from me, doubt is what does the most damage.

If you find yourself wondering, questioning, 'Can I do this?' develop a Bob the Builder mentality and affirm to yourself, 'Yes, YOU CAN!' Ditch the self-doubt because it feeds procrastination and delays action. If you are going to doubt something, doubt your limits. Decide to have a growth mindset, adopt a CAN DO attitude it's the difference that will make the difference.

Mindfulness

Have you ever got in the car and arrived at your destination completely unaware of your journey? You are not alone. The mind tends to wander and can be captured by something that attracts its attention even when you are deliberately trying to focus on something. We can spend much of our life operating on automatic pilot reacting to people and situations without much thought or consideration.

Mindfulness is a practice that nurtures a state of relaxed alertness, which helps you to relate directly to whatever is happening both internally and externally. It involves allowing yourself to be where you are and to become more familiar with your experience of thoughts and feelings moment-by-moment rather than getting caught up reliving memories or making forecasts about your future.

So what's all this got to do with confidence?

With the practice of mindfulness you enjoy a feeling of being grounded; centred and having a sense of inner peace. Your powers of concentration and focus improve and you become more relaxed and trusting in your ability to handle things even when your confidence is wavering.

Rather than allowing your emotions to run the show, you become more conscious of your thoughts and feelings. Instead of wandering mindlessly you wonder mindfully as you become curious about the signals your body is giving you in the form of thoughts and reactions to people and circumstances in which you find yourself.

Mindfulness practice consists of different forms of meditation and movement. Since my early 20s I have found becoming mindful of my breathing to be most effective in helping me to feel more relaxed, focused and confident before exams, interviews and speaking engagements. Now 10 minutes of focused breath work throughout my day keeps me calm and confident.

It's best to do this exercise in a place where you are likely to be undisturbed and either lie down or sit upright in a chair. With practice, through time you will be able to take a martini approach to mindful breathing and do it any time, any place, anywhere.

Exercise

Once you are settled into position take a slow deep breath in through the nose (say for a count of 3 - 5) then exhale through the mouth for a count slightly longer than the inhalation.

Do at least ten rounds of this in the beginning and gradually increment in blocks of five until you reach about 20 minutes.

If your mind wanders that's ok, just acknowledge your thoughts you can say out loud or internally 'thinking' and without judgment let them go and refocus on your breath.

On occasions when I have been particularly anxious especially during the night I have found it helpful to say the following phrase:

On inhalation, "All is well…" On exhalation. "…And all will be well." Doing this has brought me to a place of deep relaxation and peace.

There are various mindfulness meditations available in both book and digital format. I highly recommend anything by Jon Kabat-Zinn and offer details of his books and others for further reading in the resource section.

'A' right state or 'the' right state

Having a growth mindset doesn't stop you getting your knickers into a twist when you are faced with a situation that has the fear factor for you. It might be a speaking engagement, a date, an interview, a networking event or a party. Whatever the circumstances, your self-talk might be of a negative manner and you're possibly picturing all sorts of disasters happening in your head.

If a similar situation went wrong in the past then there is a good chance that you are still strongly associating with that situation and playing the fears forward. Now self-talk and mind movies are powerful skills but they become harmful if you are employing them unconsciously in a negative way to fuel fears that demise your confidence. Think about what could happen if we started using these skills to work for you rather than against you.

One of my clients was tormented by negative self-talk regarding a forthcoming sales pitch she was to make to a potential client. She spent many a restless night with that nagging, mocking voice ringing in her ears.

"Who do you think you are?"

"You're not experienced enough."

"They'll laugh you out the door."

… blah, blah, blah, on and on it went.

During our session, I asked Louise if she might tell me where the voice was located in her body, she replied it was at her right temple I asked her to imagine a switch at the side of her head and asked her to turn the volume down. On doing so she said she felt a little better but the voice was still there. I then asked her to move the voice to the left temple and to soften the pitch and turn the volume way down low. She felt a lot better and when she moved the voice a foot way outside of her Louise was able to critically assess the truth of these tormenting statements and realised they were nonsense. With this intervention as well as some mindfulness exercises she was able to make her pitch with ease and confidence and succeeded in making the sale.

I worked with Louise to make changes to her auditory experience by changing the distance, tone and volume of the internal dialogue. You can do the same with negative images that you hold in your mind...

- Put the movie on a big screen in your mind's eye.
- Run the movie in black and white.
- Now turn it into sepia; that grey/brown colour like an old photograph.
- Make it darker still and move it further away from you.
- Take the movie out of focus slightly so that the images become unclear.
- Now start to shrink the movie on the screen until it finally becomes a white dot.

Doing this with your mind movie helps you to show yourself that the scenario is in the past and is not happening now and therefore will have less impact on your confidence.

The right state

Our memories are stored as associations with our senses. Have you noticed when you hear a certain piece of music you think of a specific person or time in your life which can lead to a range of emotions happy, sad to name a few. In Neuro Linguistic Programming, which is the study of excellence, it is said that any external stimulus that triggers an internal state or response is known as an anchor.

Anchors are a great way to help you build confidence because you can use all of your positive experiences and memories to help you become more resourceful in the future.

You can do this using the following steps:

1 **Get really clear about the positive state you want to be in and be clear and specific in the words you use to describe it.**
E.g. your confident state maybe relaxed and alert or charming and witty.

2 **Recall a specific occasion from the past when you have been in that state.**
The context can be different but the experience comparable.

3 **Engage fully with that past experience.**
See what you saw, hear what you heard, feel what you felt; physical feelings and internal sensations.

Having followed the above steps you are in the highest possible state to set an anchor and you can do this by squeezing the thumb and first finger of either hand together.

Now when you need to get back into a positive state, you simply fire the anchor for yourself by squeezing the thumb and first finger together.

Compile a Confidence Treasure Chest

I, and many of my clients, have found it helpful to create a confidence treasure chest.

Get a box and decorate it or buy one already decorated and start to put in mementoes of your success such as photos of times when you looked and felt great. My confidence treasure chest contains childhood certificates and medals from tap and Irish dancing competitions, my qualification certificates, photos of when I looked and felt at my best, and photos of when I perhaps didn't look my best because I'd run a 10k but felt 'grrrrrreat', copies of the first talk I gave which was well received, references and recommendations and of course my confidence resume.

A Confidence Resume

There is nothing quite like taking an inventory of your success in all areas of your life to get a clearer perspective of yourself and self-worth. I've done this exercise on hundreds of occasions with clients, and in workshops, and it never fails to amaze me how people fail to see their achievements or their gifts.

In a recent workshop, a woman struggled to see her achievements or what her greatest contributions were. She was genuinely stuck and blind to herself. With a little digging we uncovered that she had abseiled down Glasgow University Tower to raise a considerable amount of money for charity. She had raised three children on her own, recently passed her driving test, was very successful in her role as a learning support assistant in a secondary school. Once we uncovered these she was on a roll and amazed herself and her colleagues who were dumbfounded by her achievements, but more so by her failure to recognise, share and celebrate them. Her attitude was one of 'so what' but through discussion she realised that not everyone could do what she did. Because it was easy for her, she failed to recognise and value her skills, talents and personal attributes; care, kindness and compassion for the pupils in her care and her colleagues.

The chances are you too are overlooking your uniqueness and a lot of what comes easy to you. You have possibly forgotten all that you have achieved. Take this opportunity to see yourself with fresh eyes and complete your confidence resume.

To construct your confidence resume I suggest you review your life and reflect on your achievements. You might find it useful to do this in 5-10 year periods and consider the following questions:

- What where your confidence highs and lows during this time?
- What significant events would you include?
- What insights and learning can you take from those times?

- List at least five achievements that made you feel good about yourself.

Now think about how your confidence has changed over time and how past events have shaped your life. If similar circumstances were to present themselves again how might you handle them now?

Think about what you have going for you now.

- What new opportunities are being presented to you?
- How might your experience to date prepare you for these opportunities?

When you have finished this exercise add it to your treasure chest, review it regularly, and remember to keep adding mementoes too.

Generosity and Gratitude

You may be wondering what generosity and gratitude have got to do with confidence, but actually it has a lot and tells you a considerable amount about a person. When a person operates from a place of scarcity or lack they are subconsciously telling themselves there is not enough and that they may be incapable of creating more of what they want in life, whether it be money or love or anything else for that matter. From a Universal Law perspective that's exactly what they attract.

When one comes from a place of abundance, you trust that the Universe will provide for you and have confidence in your ability to survive and thrive. You have an attitude of prosperity consciousness knowing that you have enough. This awareness makes it easier for you to give.

I am not suggesting for one moment that you make a pauper of yourself in order to let others prosper. I've already pointed out the importance of giving to yourself first before giving to another. However knowing that in life and work you get what you give and that the Law of Reciprocity is always at work, even though it isn't always instantaneous, builds confidence. Start with a smile and see how it comes back to you.

An attitude of gratitude also helps to build confidence because you start to realise and truly appreciate your skills, gifts and talents. You recognise your own magnificence and that builds self-confidence and others confidence in you.

Genuinely be grateful for and to the people who support and love you, see the gifts in your challenges. Now I understand that at the time these gifts are often difficult to see, but challenges do contain lessons that we can learn to appreciate. When we count our blessing we come to realise how prosperous we really are and as our appreciation grows so we attract more blessings to us and in turn authentic confidence develops.

Keep a gratitude journal. Invest in a notebook; something colourful and rich and each evening record the gifts you've received each day and watch the number grow.

Create your own Confidence Council

Get yourself a courageous council. Identify a group of people who you know will love and support you through the good times and bad. You need to have a Number 1 Fan, someone to cheer you when you're down and doubting yourself. Someone who thinks you're the bee's knees and believes in you 100%, a critical friend who will challenge your thinking and assumptions to make sure you've considered all the pros and cons so that you can make informed decisions. Get yourself a mentor - someone who has been there and done what you want to achieve. Learn from their experience and model what they do. Learn about their beliefs and attitudes towards the area you want to succeed in. Your personal support team are vital to your confidence and success. No-one can do it alone. Even Jesus had 12 Apostles!

Summary

- Developing a growth mindset means you allow yourself to believe that your abilities can be developed through persistence, dedication and hard work.

- Mindfulness is a practice that nurtures a state of relaxed alertness, which helps you to relate directly to whatever is happening both internally and externally, it allows you to live more presently rather than focusing on the past or the future.

- You can get yourself in to 'a' right state or '**the**' right state the choice is yours.

- Taking an inventory of your success in all areas of your life gives you a clearer perspective of yourself and self-worth.

- Identify a group of people who you know will love and support you through the good times and bad.

- Attitudes of generosity and gratitude say a lot about a person's confidence.

Chapter 7 - Your Word is Your Wand or Is It?

'It's not what you say that matters. It is where you speak from within yourself that counts. It is not what you hear, it is where you listen from within yourself that gives meaning to the message'.

Iyanla Vanzant

In this chapter, we are going to be looking at affirmations, what they are and what has to happen to make them work.

Before I began my personal development journey, I had used affirmations successfully in my life to attract what I desired without realising what I was doing. Let me give you an example, when I had aspirations of becoming a Principal Teacher I would walk about the house pretending I was introducing myself to staff and parents. "Hello, please to meet you, I'm Anne McGhee, Principal Teacher of Guidance."

Interestingly enough though, when I became conscious of affirmations through personal development books I didn't quite get the same success rate, which confused me quite a bit and sent me off on an investigation and exploration of what was going on and why it was going wrong. During this study I uncovered a truth and wisdom that I now share.

I get many emails from women telling me they are affirming day and night yet things still haven't changed for them. I know exactly where they are coming from because I was making the same mistakes when constructing my affirmations because I was unaware of the spiritual laws and how they work. Once you come to know and understand spiritual law and appreciate it works indiscriminately, you become much more mindful of where you focus your attention, what you say and how you say it. It is this knowledge and understanding of the power of words that enables you to attract and affirm correctly.

So what exactly is an affirmation and why don't they always work?

Thought, word and deed are the three levels of creation. The Spiritual Law of Affirmation states that you bring about what you affirm, so if you think or say something enough times you will see it manifest in your physical reality. That's because thoughts or words constantly repeated enter the unconscious mind and become part of your programming.

Most people are not mindful of their thoughts and self-talk, without realising where their focus is they are constantly using the Laws of Attention and Affirmation to attract more of what they don't want into their life.

You see the unconscious mind is like a computer, and accepts all input without discrimination, it doesn't compute negatives it simply ignores them. Now, I was reminded of this teaching recently, not being mindful of my language or thoughts I was affirming that, 'I don't want to live in this apartment anymore', which was entering my unconscious mind without the 'don't' as 'I want to live in this apartment'. Months and months went by without a property of interest appearing on the market. When I became aware of what I was doing I changed my affirmation to, 'I'm ready to move', and started clearing out in preparation, shortly afterwards I was out viewing properties 2 or 3 times a week.

Equally, by thinking you want something for example, 'I want to feel more confident', 'I want success', 'I want a relationship' the universe will bring the direct manifestation of your thoughts and feelings, which is the continued 'wanting' of whatever it is you desire. Think about it, that's why you are waiting so long for it to show up in your life, the feeling you have is one of longing for, right?

So what's the best way to affirm?

Affirmations must be kept simple, said in the present tense and with passion. If you affirm that you are going to be fit and healthy tomorrow, tomorrow never comes. It is better to affirm, 'I am fit and healthy now'. Passion and belief contain positive vibes, which are powerfully attractive so never, make affirmations half-heartedly, expect the best and leave the rest to the universe.

To create your own affirmations start by taking some time to think about the areas in your life you would like to improve and how you might want your life to be. It is worth taking some time over this process.

- Write the most important ones down in a list.
- Now look at each item on the list and write out a few positive statements for each, remember to focus on what you **do** want, not on what you don't want.

Affirmations, which are rhyming or rhythmic, slip into your unconscious mind easily. The following example is an affirmation for instilling self-confidence and self-honour and is from Diana Cooper's book, *A Time for Transformation*.

'Calm and centred, quiet and still. I love myself and always will'.

An affirmation is not based on what you know now it is something you grow into, so when you affirm you must believe that what you are saying is possible for you. Affirmations must not threaten any belief, which outright denies present experience.

For example, if you are currently affirming 'I'm a millionaire' when you are in dire straits financially it's too much of a leap for the mind to make and your likely to hear a little voice say, "Come on now, who you kidding? Get real!"

What is needed is the kind of affirmation that will enable the mind to be intrigued and which doesn't fly in the face of current reality. An example might be, 'The Universe is the source of all my supply', or, 'I am the centre of abundance. I am a magnet of prosperity'. Rather than resistance, you are more likely to get a, 'Mmm that's interesting, let's see what happens now', response from the mind. After several repetitions you will begin to feel more at peace and trusting, as well as better able to focus on the new belief.

Ask and you shall receive

Noah St. John, Success Mentor and author of *The Great Little Book of Afformations* suggests rather than making a statement you don't believe, ask yourself a question. By doing so your mind automatically begins to search for an answer without your conscious volition. The trick is to ask empowering questions rather than disempowering questions.

Disempowering questions come from a place of fear, focus on what you lack and what's wrong with you. They speak from your pain making you feel yucky and stuck because as the Law of Attraction states what you continually focus on will grow and bear fruit.

Read the following questions out loud:

- Why am I so unhappy?
- Why don't I have enough?
- Why am I so lonely?'

Feeling good? Didn't think so!

Now for the next few hours I want you to listen to what you say to yourself when you talk to yourself. Sit with this for a bit, you might even want to leave completing the following exercise for a day or two, during that time just be mindful of 'the voice' what it's saying and how it's saying it. When you are ready answer the following question on the next page:

When you talk to yourself what are three disempowering questions you ask?

_____

_____

_____

Empowering questions on the other hand lead your mind to focus on what you have, what's right about you and come from a place of power.

Read these questions out loud:

- Why am I so successful?
- Why do I have enough?
- Why am I loved so much?

Did you notice the intriguing pause and how quickly the mind jumped from confusion to questioning to seeking clarity and confirmation? Did you notice the, 'Mmm that's interesting', thought coming into play? Are you thinking more positively? Feeling good about yourself?

Now reverse the negative questions you wrote above to positive ones.

_____

_____

_____

Remember to ask these questions of yourself on a regular basis, you may want to write them out on card and put them in places where you can regularly look at them.

Confident behaviour comes from hidden, unconscious assumptions about how life is going to treat you. When you think life is on your side you take action from a place of faith believing that things will work out for the best and the results will naturally follow. When you come from a place of fear or lack, your expectations are negative and the results you get will meet your expectations – it's universal law.

The point of this method is not to find the answer to your question but to change what your mind automatically focuses on and to take action based on your new assumptions about life. So mind your language both internally and externally, when you hear yourself make negative statements or questions turn them in to positive affirmations or empowering questions.

Whilst, I do believe your word is your wand. I think it's also important to remember thought, word and deed are the three levels of creation. I didn't just affirm myself in to the role of Principal Teacher of Guidance. I spoke about my aspirations within my professional network and I got the necessary experience by taking on a pupil caseload. I attended training courses, engaged in professional reading and dialogue with colleagues and was mentored by an experienced Principal Teacher.

However, I do believe that the constant repetition of the above phrase and talking with others about my aspirations, created opportunities for me and helped me believe it was only a matter of time before it happened.

I still use affirmations today but I always back them up with appropriate action.

Summary

- The process of speech creates.

- The Spiritual Law of Affirmation states that you bring about what you affirm, so if you think or say something enough times you will see it manifest in your physical reality.

- An affirmation is not based on what you know now it is something you grow into, so when you affirm you must believe that what you are saying is possible for you.

- Affirmations must be kept simple, said with passion in the present tense and focus on what you want not what you don't want.

- Rather than making a statement you don't believe, you can ask yourself an empowering question.

- Confident behaviour comes from hidden, unconscious assumptions about how life is going to treat you.

- Mind your language! Watch what you say to yourself about yourself and question if what others say about you is true.

- When you hear yourself make negative statements or questions turn them in to positive affirmations or an empowering question. But remember thought, word and deed are the three levels of creation.

Affirmations for Authentic Confidence

Sometimes coming up with the right words for your own affirmations can be a bit of a challenge. The following affirmations resonated with me in my quest to close the confidence competence gap and they focus on many of the themes we've covered in this book. Take what resonates with you and feel free to tweak until you feel at ease with them because it is the sense of ease with the words that will ignite the power within you to say them with purpose and passion.

Along with the learning and insights you've gained through previous chapters these affirmations will bring you to a place of self-acceptance, self-love and authenticity, a place where confidence resides within.

Awareness

- Each day I become more aware of my talents and abilities.
- Every day I become more aware of the world around me.
- I am forever aware of the words I say to myself and to others.
- I am consciously aware of what I am thinking, feeling and believing.

Belief

- All my beliefs are in harmony with my goals.
- Because of my empowering beliefs, I know that anything is possible.

- I am now recreating myself, one positive belief at a time.
- Every day I replace past limiting beliefs with new empowering ones.

Confidence

- Absolute authentic confidence blesses every day of my life.
- Every day I am become more and more self-assured.
- Everything I do is right for me.

Commitment

- Absolutely nothing can stop me from realizing my dreams.
- All of my actions support my intentions.
- I am always true to the commitments I make.
- I am committed to becoming the best I can be.
- I can do it, I am doing it!

Deservability

- I love and approve of myself, I deserve the very best in life and I am open to receiving it.
- Every day I appreciate myself more and more.

Love

- I know that I deserve love and accept it now.
- I give out love and it is returned to me multiplied.
- I rejoice in the love I encounter everyday.

Self Esteem

- When I believe in myself, so do others.
- I express my needs and feelings.
- I am my own unique self - special, creative and wonderful.
- By loving myself, I allow others to love me as well.

Trust

- I release the past and now embrace a trusting attitude.
- I trust myself and I trust in the process of life.
- Life supplies all my needs in abundance, I trust in life.
- I trust my vibes.

Uniqueness

- I accept my uniqueness.
- I am perfect exactly as I am, I celebrate and honour my uniqueness.
- Freedom is mine when I express my individuality.

Chapter 8 - Can you? YOU CAN!

'Success comes in cans not cant's'.

Author Unknown

If I were to ask you right now, "What's getting in the way of you being, doing or having what you want most in life?" You are most likely to provide a 'Can't' response that includes an external factor such as time, money, commitments and obligations. What I'd like to suggest is that what has really been stopping you until now, is an internal factor such as deservability, permission or self-love because when you possess each of these you possess confidence within.

Deservability

Deservabilty is a tough nut to crack because we've been taught to feel it through childhood experiences of learning to make do or settling for less than we wanted. We've also learned it through religious guilt and the secret shames we hold deep inside from past experiences gone wrong. It's often influenced by the thought that if we really deserved to have what we desire then it would have happened by now. But your ability to use the Law of Attraction to manifest what it is you want in life is an inside job.

The universe is delivering your desires (or not) according to your own sense of worth and deservability. If, at the deepest core of your being, you don't feel you deserve to have what you wish for, that belief will block those things from coming into your life. Once you come to appreciate that it's your birthright to be successful, whatever that personally means to you, and once you realise that the universe wants you to have your deepest desires, dreams can come true.

Once you recognise that you have a valuable contribution to make in this life, that you are here for a purpose and you are clear on what that purpose is, not only do you attract opportunities to you, but you take the opportunity presented rather than reject it through fear of not being good enough.

Now this is going to sound a little crazy but there have been times in the past when I rejected work because I thought I wasn't good enough to do it. Early in my coaching career I was approached by a Director of large banking institution to coach a group of female executives but I redirected the request to another coach because I wasn't sure I was going to be able to do it. It wasn't a time issue it was a 'CAN DO' issue, I made excuses to myself about these women being far more successful than me, so how could I support them? What could they learn from me? I had attracted the opportunity, I wanted it but rejected it because I didn't feel worthy of it.

In the past I've done that with other aspects of my life attracting 'my ideal man' - tall, dark, handsome, intelligent, spiritual, successful in his own career who made me laugh and I could be myself with. But I pushed him away because I was scared of getting hurt and couldn't see why he would be attracted to me. I felt unworthy of him, not tall enough, not glamorous enough, how could I be his type? I didn't allow myself or him to discover otherwise. I didn't stop to wonder if he was good enough for me. Is this something that you do?

To help you get clear about your deservability you need to get personal with your mission, your vision and your motivation. The following exercise will help you do this as well as provide you with an opportunity to reflect on where any deservability issues may have arisen from and, consequently, help you resolve them.

Exercise

Your Mission

- Who am I?
- What do I stand for? What is important to me?

Your Vision

- What do I want that I don't have now?

Your Motivation

- Why is this important to me?
- What do you have to live for? What is the purpose of your life?

Deservability

- What did you learn about deserving in your childhood?

- Do you feel that you are deserving of good things, or do you feel that you have to do something to earn them? Are you good enough?

- What do you deserve? Do you believe: "I deserve love and joy and all good"?

- Or do you feel deep down that you deserve nothing? Are you willing to let go of your limiting beliefs about deservability?

Remember you only need to be willing to let go of your limiting beliefs about your deservability to start the process. You might find the following passage helpful to read regularly.

Deservability Treatment

I am deserving. I deserve the best in every way.
I deserve good health.
I deserve the best career, doing a job that I love and that I am very well paid for.
I deserve the best relationship, one that is loving and nurturing where I am heard and seen.
I deserve love on every level.
I deserve freedom to be all that I can be.
I move past all restricting and negative thoughts.
I let go of the limitations of my parents. I love them, and I go beyond them.
I am not their negative opinions or their limiting beliefs.
I am not bound by any of the fears or prejudices of the society in which I live. I no longer identify with limitations of any kind.
I attract only the best to me.
I attract my Highest Good and my Greatest Joy to me NOW. Right NOW not tomorrow or next week...NOW!
For, I am deserving.
I accept it and I know it to be true.

Permission

From a very early age we are taught to ask for 'permission' before we take action, for example permission to ask a question in class, permission to leave the table, permission to stay out late or go on a date. If what we want to have or do, will significantly affect others around us then it is reasonable for us to seek their permission before proceeding. But many times we consciously, or unconsciously, seek permission from others because we are not sure it is 'OK' for us to have or do what we want or because we feel we do not "deserve" what we want.

Sarah has a passion for shoes and bought a pair of Jimmy Choo's. She has a great social life and attends many balls and fancy functions but she never wears her Choo's. Instead she keeps them in a box in her wardrobe and occasionally takes them out to admire them or for a walk around the carpeted floors of her home. Whilst Sarah has given herself permission to buy expensive and beautiful things she hasn't given herself permission to actually enjoy wearing the shoes and risk damaging them even though she could she could probably afford to buy another pair.

Alison came from a family of teachers but since her early teens she had dreamed of running her own business but had gone straight in to teacher training as a safe employment option after graduating from university. She swiftly worked her way up the ladder to headship of a primary school and whilst she was very good at her job and it was rewarding enough, she still felt unfulfilled and harboured dreams of entrepreneurship. Alison held herself back from taking the big leap for fear of leaving her comfort zone and failing. No one was telling her she ought to live her dream and because she was unable to give herself permission to experiment with her life, change career and start her own business she remained unfulfilled in teaching.

What these real life examples demonstrate is that while we may know what we want to do or have in our lives, we often find ourselves drawn to look outside ourselves for the permission to pursue it or the permission that says that we are good enough. The problem with seeking permission from others is that it robs you of your own personal power and your full potential.

Giving yourself permission is just a matter of making a decision. Go within and listen to your inner wisdom, get a sense of what it's telling you, check in with your feelings. Be mindful of the language you use when you talk about the decision to be made because these are clear indicators of whether you should be making a decision in the moment or not.

I have personally found it very helpful to follow the advice of one of my mentors David Neagle, Success and Wealth Consciousness Coach, who offers four questions for your reflection.

1. Is this opportunity something that I want to be, do or have?
A simple yes or no answer is all that is required to this question. If you want the opportunity then you move on to question two otherwise the decision is made and you let the opportunity go.

2. Is being, doing or having this going to take me closer to my goal / heart's desire / life's purpose?
Again a simple yes or no answer is all that's required, if the answer is no again let it go.

3. Is being, doing or having this in harmony with the laws of the universe?
For an opportunity to be in harmony with the laws of the universe it would have to add to your life without taking away from someone else's which is further clarified by question 4.

4. Is being, doing or having this going to violate the rights of others?
By embracing the opportunity, would you be taking away another person's ability to choose?

If you answered *yes* to the first three questions and *no* to the fourth question, then the universe will support you in moving forward. Whatever it is that you need in terms of resources, people or support will start to flow towards you, but first you must make the decision and trust that the way and the 'how to' will become clear.

When I decided to set up my own business I knew that I couldn't afford to retain the flat that I was living in so I made the decision to sell it. It was October and I expected to be living there until the following January at least. My flat sold within 2 days of being on the market. I was shocked and scared because I had to be out within 6 weeks and if I'm honest, heartbroken too because I loved that flat and thought I wouldn't get anything better in my price range. My focus was on finding a rented property fast. I saw a few dodgy dwellings but without too much effort I found a flat a little more expensive than I'd planned for but well worth it as it was even better than the one I'd left. It had a terrace, underground parking and concierge service. Shortly after I settled in to the flat business began to flow.

When you do not love yourself and suffer from low self-esteem, it is almost impossible to ever reach the potential that you suspect you have. Recognising you deserve to have what you want and giving yourself permission to go after it, is an act of self-love. Learning to love yourself starts with making a conscious decision, an intention to become happy and lead a fulfilled life.

Self-love

I want to clarify here the difference between self-love and 'lov'n yourself' a phrase often used by we Glaswegians to describe someone who is over confident or perhaps has narcissistic tendencies. Social philosopher and Psychologist Erich Fromm proposed that loving oneself is different from being arrogant, conceited or egocentric. He proposed that loving oneself means caring about oneself, taking responsibility for oneself and the outcomes we create. It's about self-respect and self-knowledge, and being realistic and honest about one's strengths and weaknesses. He proposed, further, that in order to be able to truly love another person, a person needs first to love oneself in this way. It's not an easy process. I've been through it but the inner peace and contentment it brings is pure gold.

Self-love involves recognizing that you are constantly evolving to become more powerful and more loving. It's about no longer settling for what is but recognising what you can become. By accepting the invitation to grow that this book offers, you are telling your unconscious mind and the universe that you want more, you deserve more and you are open to receiving and willing to do the work to get it. Much of the work you have covered in this book is an act of self-love because you have invested money, time and effort to get to know yourself and you have found reasons and ways to like and trust yourself. I urge you to continue your journey of self-discovery, self-development and self-love because that commitment will facilitate the development of confidence within - an authentic confidence which is a very powerful place to operate from.

And finally...

We reach the C of authentic confidence, which stands for **Commitment**. After all the work you have done in this book I'm inviting you to make a commitment to yourself. Commit to seeing and being the woman you really are, rather than hiding away. Become a seeker of the gold that lies within you, become curious about who you might become, what you are capable of doing and what if... you had all your hearts desires. Curiosity leads to creatively finding ways to manifest whatever you want but remember you have to be really clear about what you want and believe you are worthy of receiving it. And you are, aren't you?

Commit to being courageous in communicating what you want and more importantly what you don't want. Speak what's in your heart rather than what's on your mind. Remember the Law of Attraction works on many levels. Doing things because you 'have to' holds you in bondage so be mindful of your boundaries and commit to honouring yourself. Confidence comes with action so give process to the Law of Attraction. Commit to taking small successful steps to magnetize what you want to you. Create, Focus, Believe, Achieve and if at any point you are suffering from self-doubt STOP and believe in my belief in you because I know you CAN DO it!

Love & blessings

Anne x

Summary

- Deservability, allowing and self-love are key to authentic confidence.

- Giving yourself permission is just a matter of making a decision to allow yourself to have, be and do what you want.

- Self-love means caring about oneself, taking responsibility for oneself and the outcomes we create. It's about self-respect and self-knowledge, and being realistic and honest about one's strengths and weaknesses.

- The C of authentic confidence stands for becoming conscious of your greatness, committing to honouring yourself and being courageous in taking action because action builds confidence.

- Whatever you want you can be it, you can have it. You CAN DO it!

Recommended Reading and Resources

James Allen, *As A Man Thinketh*.
Martha Beck, *Finding Your Own North Star*.
Claude M Bristol, *The Magic of Believing*.
Pema Chodron, *The Wisdom of No Escape*.
Deepak Chopra, *The Seven Spiritual Laws of Success*.
Diana Cooper, *A Little Light on the Spiritual Laws*.
Jill Edwards, *Living Magically*.
Esther and Jerry Hicks, Ask and It Is Given: *Learning to Manifest the Law of Attraction*.
Esther and Jerry Hicks, *The Law of Attraction: How to Make It Work For You*.
Jon Kabat-Zinn, *Full Catastrophe Living: How to cope with stress, pain and illness using mindfulness meditation*.
Jon Kabat-Zinn, *Guided Mindfulness Meditation. (CD)*
Jon Kabat-Zinn, *Mindfuness for Beginners*.
Louise Hay, *You Can Heal Your Life*.
Raymond Holliwell, *Working with the Law*.
David Neagle. *www.davidneagle.com*.
Clarissa Pinkola Estes, *Women Who Run With The Wolves*.
Matthieu Ricard, *The Art of Meditation*.
Neil Donald Walsh, *Conversations with God: An Uncommon Dialogue Books 1 & 2..*
Neil Donald Walsh, *Happier than God*
Altazar Rossiter, *Developing Spiritual Intelligence*.
Debbie Shapiro, *Your Body Speaks Your Mind*.
Noah St John, *The Great Little Book of Afformations*.
Eckhart Tolle, *The Power of Now*.
Thich Nhat Hanh *The Miracle Of Mindfulness: The Classic Guide to Meditation by the World's Most Revered Master*.

About the Author

Anne McGhee is The CAN DO Coach for Women. She has helped countless women rediscover their authentic confidence and create happy, fulfilling and successful lives and careers. Over the last 15 years, Anne has worked with Private and Public Sector organisations helping their people achieve their aspirations and enjoy success by being themselves.

Anne is a sought after speaker and has featured in the national press. To request a speaking engagement or to receive information on coaching programmes or events email admin@annemcghee.com

A Request From Anne McGhee

I'd love to hear your success stories and any feedback you may have about this book. I am a woman on a mission and I want women world wide to recognise their uniqueness and worth. To be successful in being and by being their authentic selves. To become a member of the Confidence Within community and receive weekly tips on how to grow with authentic confidence in you personal and professional life visit www.annemcghee.com. You will also receive my complimentary gift to you.

With thanks and best wishes

Anne x

Also from MX Publishing

Business in Red Shoes – Rebecca Jones

"I wish this book had been available when I first set up in business. Unlike similar books Rebecca's book engaged me. It is practical and a doing book rather than talking at me. I loved the way it guides the reader to think about what kind of business would best suit their experiences and lifestyle. There are lots of gems in this book based on both Rebecca and her clients experiences. Rebecca takes you on a journey so start at the beginning. I would recommend this book not only to women thinking about going solo but also those who have already set up a business."
Women In Business

Also from MX Publishing

Stepping Into Success – Julie Johnson

Julie's passion and expertise shine through in this
refreshing business book which turns traditional business
building and business development on its head using a
unique and feminine approach that gets to the heart and
soul of success for you as a business woman.
Julie's innovative DANCE system shows you how to
create meaningful and authentic success in your business
and in your life. DANCE is a simple and creative
approach to grow your business in a completely different
way.

Also from MX Publishing

Influencing The Interview – Chris Delaney

This book isn't for the faint hearted, the 73 rules to influence the interview have taken the best from psychology, NLP and uncovered the secrets that master influencers, successful pick-up artists, powerful business leaders and notorious con artists use to get whatever they desire.

Also from MX Publishing

Engaging NLP Series – Judy Bartkowiak

"NLP is Neuro Linguistic Programming. The author is an
NLP Master Practitioner who has specialised training in
working with children. This book is an excellent
introduction to the topic, written in easily accessible
language and giving all the basic information needed to
apply the principles. I like the way the book encourages
you to write down your goals at the beginning, thus giving
positive aims and a way to measure success. It is a very
positive book which will give parents the confidence they
need to apply the ground rules outlined. These ground
rules underpin all the techniques learnt in the book and are
explained clearly and concisely. An excellent introduction
to NLP"
Parents In Touch

Lightning Source UK Ltd.
Milton Keynes UK
UKOW040743020912

198345UK00001B/15/P